THE LONGEST BREATH

Poems

by

Greg Field

THE MID-AMERICA PRESS, INC.
WARRENSBURG, MISSOURI

ACKNOWLEDGEMENTS

Present or previous versions of these poems have appeared as follows:

"The Sea Is The Longest Breath"....*New Letters* and *Spreading The Word: Editors on Poetry*, The Bench Press.

"Arshile Gorky Avoids The War" and "My Family Has Arshile Gorky for Dinner"....*The Laurel Review*.

"Nothing And No One," "After Watching A Man Playing With His Dog In The Grass," and "In The Waiting Room"....*New Letters*.

"Your Small Fingers And Their Small Bones" and "Giving Away The Night"....*Karamu*.

"On A Cold Evening Alone, I Turn On My Electric Blanket" and "A Reason To Keep Driving" ....*Kansas City Outloud II*, BookMark Press.

"Just Before Sleep"....*Potpourri Magazine*.

Cover Design by Greg Field
Illustrations by Andrea Brookhart

Financial assistance for this project has been provided by the Missouri Arts Council, a state agency.

missouri arts council

This book is for my wife, Maryfrances Wagner, who helped hone the work in this book until it was fit for publication.

In memory of Crystal MacLean Field, and Kenneth E. Field

Thanks to Robert Stewart, who helped me refine some
of the earlier poems, and to Father Edward Hays
and the staff at Shantivanam; within its peace
I wrote several of these poems.

The Longest Breath
is the winner
of
The Mid-America Press, Inc.,
Writing Award for 1997

CONTENTS

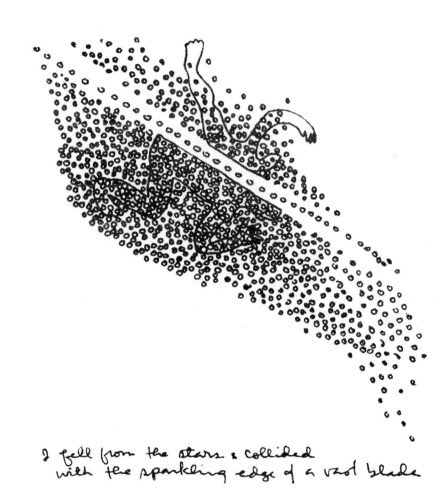

I fell from the stars & collided
with the sparkling edge of a vast blade

THE SEA IS THE LONGEST BREATH

for Crystal

The sea is the longest breath ever taken.
Its vast green chest rises again
before it can completely fall—
forever pumped by wind and moon.
This sailboat's engine is like
the biggest heart that ever beat,
its rhythm so strong the bulkheads hum.
Between this heart and that breath
a song drifts out over the sea.
It is the longest song ever sung.
It goes on for days,
passed on from hull to waves,
as we plunge and heave and roll
across the sea's nervous chest.
This song is for you.
Now you are the sea, the wind,
the moon and the song
that rises up to sting my eyes,
to coat my hair in salt.
Sing on past the time
the boat rests sluggish in its slip,
on softly to my ears at night
when I am alone,
into my dreams where we both
stand on deck before I awaken
and you turn to me to say,
the sea is the longest breath ever taken.

WHERE WE MUST LIVE

There is nothing so ancient,
nothing so pure as purpose,
but the purpose of your dreams
is not to save you.
No hawk will carry you
across the night, to the moon,
to the sharp stars.
No cat will guard the door
of the hollow house,
nor go before any gods
to speak in your behalf.
The purpose of the stories
is not to collect the animals,
the totems, the strong hearts.
The stories are pictures
to sigh over, their purpose,
to line the inside of your head
like the skins
on your childhood's walls.
Your soul won't catch directions
till later, it will miss the way
the earth's turning directs you
around its curve to the sunset,
where you belong above waves,
in the dense rolling air,
where you must live.

ALL WE'RE WORTH

There is more light
than the unconscious will ever need.
I hold the hand of someone
I love; she lies
on a cold steel gurney.
This room is smaller
and then smaller.
It echoes the discourse
of the nurses' desk, catalog
of the maladies of those before us.
Everyone dies from love or money
while searching for spare parts.

We are one couple in an unfolding history
of couples, gurneys, and hands being held.
We hear humor whispered in the hall
and it seems to tug
at our intern's eyes as if
he were missing something.
The sheets are too thin.
The instruments are down the hall.
This leaves time to draw blood,
to think about the worst.

Each of us has our turn,
has our trust tried.
We have ourselves,
our hands to touch
and hold the promises
we cannot keep,
and all we're worth
before we sleep.

IN THE WAITING ROOM

I was still too late.
Put in the waiting room—
me, an unfinished form,
my hopes, my address blank.
They offered reports,
so I never saw you
and searched for a way.
I collected blood in my belly,
spilled it into my lungs,
coughed it out—a mist
so fine only I saw it.
It traveled through halls and walls
to where you lay dying.
But tubes, a mask kept it out—
then a surgeon removed
an arterial catheter.
My blood got in
only to be forced out
by the simple-minded push
of your damaged heart.
Both of us did what we must.
The system had locked you in
to the speeding stars
and tumble of this galaxy.
My eyes saw the darkness
that is the motor of all things.
My body gave in. My lungs
emptied for air.
My eyes were too dry to see
that nothing can save these
beautiful assemblies
of meat and bone.
Not blood, not love.

IDENTIFYING THE DEAD

I

A formality, the doctor said.
you don't have to go, and then,
don't go alone, and so I went.
I identified my wife
in a big ice-cold room
with large, plastic plants
and a display of new caskets.
She lay on a gurney draped with cloth.
A woman at the door wouldn't leave.
She was afraid of my unshaven face
and my request to be left alone.

II

Not long after, I went back
to my inner-city classroom
to try to be the teacher I had been.
I took to standing alone
in empty stairwells on breaks.
One afternoon, a student leaped down
onto my back to beat my head
with his small black fists.
For a while, I stumbled under his weight,
for a while I felt nothing.
Then, with each blow I saw the gurney,
the cheap cloth, felt the icy air
sharp in my eyes and gazed down
the way my dog gazes at his empty water bowl
in the violent August heat.
I gazed down into the empty stainless bowl
and then knocked the weight from my shoulders.

III

Not long after I watched
the faintest silver flash
of my wife's ashes wink out
below the rolling green sea,
a woman visitor stayed late.
She asked me if I wanted
her to sleep with me.
Like my wife, she was generous,
though when I held her,
only her skin held me.
But my ragged pieces dying each night,
she somehow rescued and returned.
When I was rebuilt, she moved
far across a river.
Later, she sent a prayer in the mail.
She wrote, *hoped it would help.*
But the river was a stronger prayer.
It carried away distance,
but replaced it with more distance.
The prayer carried away light
and replaced it with the faintest
silver flash of simple fish.

IV

After the woman left me,
I began to notice the stars.
The night sky flooded my dreams.
I saw how the stars are rooted in our flesh,
how we are rooted in their fire.
As I flailed in their space, I saw eternity;
what it was like to almost live forever,
but surrounded in darkness;

to attack everything with light;
only to be gazed upon, but never touched.

V

During these dreams I ground my teeth
trying to eat the dark space around me.
Only a formality, the dentist said,
and stuck his finger in my mouth
to probe the worn smooth enamel.
I tried to explain to him
I had been compelled to eat
what I couldn't possibly have
as I had been compelled to identify
what I could no longer love.

VI

Later, a new dream
cut its way into my sleep.
I fell from the stars and collided
with the sparkling edge of a vast blade.
From head to crotch,
I was sliced cleanly in half.
One side useless, lifeless,
the other was ushered awkwardly
into a cold, white room
and commanded to identify
the inanimate half dripping
from an old wooden gurney.
It took all night
to gather myself together.

VII

I began to forgo sleep.
to spend long hours after school
gathering and cleaning the equipment
in my silent art room.
One night I found a painting
wedged like a dirty secret under a radiator.
It carried the name of the student
who'd tried to beat me in the stairwell.
I saved it; I took it home;
I smoothed it flat and placed it under my bed.
It is a picture of crude ruptured hearts
fading into a broken black surface
surrounded by red, then blue,
then darkness out to the edges.
It is a picture of the stars;
an empty stainless bowl
carried miles toward the river;
a prayer in the mail.

...midwest stalk-stubbled field
is the winter beneath my feet.

NOTHING AND NO ONE

It's not the sun
that burns the night.
It's the fire
that burns up the blackness,
slips up the tunnel
of brick and rock built high
and maybe reaches for heaven.
But nothing and no one ever
touches what passes for god.
There is too much
darkness to burn.
It's all that's left
after the fire dies,
just the night,
the mirror of the moon.
You can look into
the caverns of the coals
where it's very hot for awhile
and flesh passes away
with the remains of the dark,
but these lights go out, too.
The cold is unbearable
like love. And love is
unbearable like the mirror.
And the mirror is unbearable
like life that burns white—
collapsing in until we find
our hearts will no longer
support us.

ACROSS THE WINTER DISTANCE

Dear friend, Midwest stalk-stubbled field
is the winter beneath my feet.
You gave up our company and the brick house
to breathe Down East air, reflect
and squint over sunny snow.
I scattered ashes beyond the Golden Gate,
returned to wander these frozen furrows.
You write your lines and sleep on love,
but my dreams are of steep green waves.
Across the winter distance I come to you
through those icy amplitudes
to bring bad news:
There is nothing that keeps us whole.
Though you thought the hundreds of blackbirds
rising from this field might be salvation,
I have seen them gather to rise again and again.
They are easily frightened.
A cloud's shadow will raise the wave of beating wings.
No, my friend, we don't escape this field,
we are rooted here, just as some of those blackbirds
will be rooted in its spring muds,
just as our love is rooted in plantings years ago
that abide and have yet to grow.

GIVING AWAY THE NIGHT

I dream the dream of my wife's return,
a dream that rides, slung across my back
like an injured, unconscious body.
It's a dream in which I've given away
all her clothes; returned the stained glass
jewelry box to her sleeping sister.
I watch my wife climb the front steps.
I know it's too dark for her
to be returning home from work.
She is smiling in the porchlight, unaware.
Will I tell her she's a misplaced orphan
like her couch I gave her cousin?
Nothing my tongue ever withheld from her
can equal this dream's truth.
It settles in my belly,
a grasping, severed hand.
Its clutching wakes me.
The nightly helicopter
has clattered over the city's edge.
Streetlights withdraw their glow
like each of her objects taken away.
On the porch, I see a wren lift up
a black twig and fly into the day.

SLEEPING WITH EYES OPEN

for Crystal

This is the world:
crisp brown petals,
cracked concrete porch,
house that settles.
This is the space:
library grounds at moon-set,
dogs free to run in damp grass,
birds just recognizing their lives.
You and I can never count
all the colors sky changed
the morning your heart died.
The appointment
to pick up the jade ring
is meaningless.
You were the space in which I moved,
asleep with eyes open.
Now the space I make
when my lips part
is only that,
and not the soft red bed
for your tongue.

CLEANING STRAWBERRIES

for Crystal

In the ripe green
pines-in-the-morning-sun,
I collect them
carefully from the garden.
Their dust muddies
the white sink
as I wash them.
Some skins break;
the meat is red
like your sunburned back
the last time
you asked me to wash it.
I trim the green crowns
from the lush red berries
and remember how you fought
to hold us all together—
letters to parents, calls
to your sister, to your son.
Now they grow ripe
in their own patches—
soft berries still hanging,
such a large collection
of flesh we are left.

SO I AM INVITED IN

Collapsed on the porch swing
I listen to an afternoon breeze chime
as it slips through shards
of dark green glass hung from a beam.
A cup of red wine and a book of poems
that keeps slipping from my hands
push me under the edge of a nap.
The distance of this shadowed atmosphere
allows me to listen to the three
big bare-chested boys build a cedar deck
next door, driving nails to anchor railings,
something solid in that outside world,
something to grasp and hold on to.
My neighbor to the south calls out
the name of her little boy.
He's wandered down the sidewalk,
vanished from the corner.
The three boys are committed
to hammer and nails and cedar.
I come doddering down my concrete steps
to help her search for the child.
Every step brings me back
until I awake three blocks west
where the boy and I find each other.
On a corner, two little girls question him
on where he comes from
and where he's headed as I intervene.
I, of necessity, am so close to these small lives.
So I am invited in, away
from a vague belief in the long lost,
bravely clutching the small proof
of his hot and sweaty hand.

lights of a semi show where
the wind has eaten a hole
in the sheets beside me.

INSIDE THE DARK CAR

There are few shadows at roadside;
most sit in here with me.
We collect them as we go.
The pavement produces no music.
The driver never speaks,
only leans and nods.
And the odor, always
the odor of alcohol
like unpredictable accident.
The spectres we pass at night
are the shadows we dropped at dusk
that wandered along the shoulder
and coalesced in the cool darkness.
How comfortable it is to breathe
as we drive on—
setting sun, rising moon.
Then a figure catches my eye.
I tip my head and the driver stops.
Outside the glass, there is someone I miss.
I roll down my window
and give her ghost a kiss.

JUST BEFORE SLEEP

A dark spot on a road's spine,
disappearing, reappearing,
as though caught between
a bird's pumping wings.
The sun, ghosted by dirty sheets
drops into a box for the blind.
The cold wind brings this
perverse flapping of old movies
beating against the windows.
Numbness seeps into the back
of the throat, down into the heart
where the motor rattles and the car
quits, too cold to fire the plugs.
Night after night, that brief roll
into silence.

A REASON TO KEEP DRIVING

for Crystal and Susan

1

There is driving, and
there is driving in a blizzard.
When the wind bashes the car across two lanes
even though my hands pull
the wheel against it, driving is
like a gun fired, and
even though you've thought to turn away
the bullet still nudges the bone
at the back of your skull.

2

The snow is a mad confectioner's
powdered sugar, it clothes the car
like icing. I can't see the moon.
Coming down into Las Cruces
snow and wind let up, give in
to expose the dark stretched out.
I think of Crystal, worry
she is lonely in the sea,
as I am, shooting under the night
listening to a lounge singer
jazz a Christmas carol on the radio.
Morning, the sun settles on the snow,
resurrects it in the sky.
I think of Susan because
she is alive.

3

Outside Deming, New Mexico,
the mountains make the clouds, and
the clouds rake over the rocks,
so sharp, they rupture,
spill more snow in confetti gusts.
Ice piles up on the side-view mirrors
'til there is no side view.
The only view is the rear
of a semi's trailer as it dully bulls
its way through rising snow,
its wheels make an awkward path
for mine all the way to Lordsburg.
I forget highways are paved.
I forget so much.

4

There is driving, and
there is driving in a blizzard.
Across the white windshield
I see a dream—
arrived home I find an angel
with wings of snow. My warm hands
touch them—they evaporate like logic.
Her arms hold me,
she says she loves my hands, and
they become the seed
of a great sea of life.

At night a cold motel room
allows the hard teeth of the wind
to eat through the door;
nibble at my edges until I'm raw.
Through the window
lights of a semi show where
the wind has eaten a hole
in the sheets beside me.

WHILE I MAKE COPIES AT KINKO'S
A GREAT SECRET IS REVEALED

Outside a man is building a wall.
Through the window I see him
in overalls only.
Mortar and stone, mortar and stone.
His assistant watches a woman
walk by in a tight black dress
soaking up the rising sun.
Mortar and stone, mortar and stone.
She's big and hot as his smile, his thoughts,
that are like gritty lines written
by the mason's trowel.
Mortar and stone, mortar and stone.
Each slide and stab of xenon light
is a point worked through my temples
not eased by lovers' fingers.
Mortar and stone, mortar and stone.
This machine's heat, like this summer day's,
is so mean the late sunset
will go unnoticed.
Mortar and stone, mortar and stone.
The counter girls sweat through thin blouses,
their breasts clutched by white cups,
hearts hidden from each other.
Mortar and stone, mortar and stone.
Across the scratched glass sky, the sun slides,
machine light and second hand glide by,
tick on to join like lovers.
Mortar and stone, mortar and stone.

THE CLEANING WOMAN

For Rita

First, she suggests a general cleaning
to get her bearings, learn the worst.
Pine cleaner, she says,
dissolves most all worries.
She finds I've been too rough
on my bathroom fixtures—
porcelain worn away in layers,
white to yellow to rust brown
to black, a complete disintegration.
I need to find a more gentle cleanser.
For a while, as she scrubs away
my deposits from the tub,
we exchange experience—
the man she lost; how she sought dust
to pay her way out of depression;
the wife I lost and the first woman after.
I am genteel now—a few woman friends
I can sip tea with but do not touch.
The cleaning woman says she is dating
a man who is big, of-a-piece, with a belly
soft as gathered fur.
She says I have put so many
memories out in the open,
they will be hard to keep up.
Her dust rag grows dark.
I tell her there will be more;
whatever is taken away, returns.
"The wind is a dupe one day,
a conspirator the next," I say,
"See what you have stirred up my friend."
Neither of us can leave this house
untouched or empty-handed.

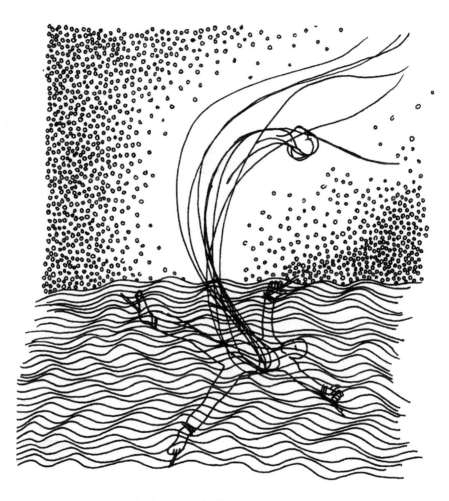

He breaks for the deck, sets free his lines;
unfurls and raises his ghost.

FALLING ASLEEP ONBOARD

From the port bunk, he watches
the masts pass by—thin, plated blades
disguised in white cloth.
He sees the breeze pester the treetops.
The sun sets gold on stanchions
and stern rails.
He's been out, bound to cut the air,
but now he's tied up,
dock line arms tug and give;
holding him to the center.
The breeze darkens and cools.
The sky looses light to the stars
and joins the water.

There was spray over the bow
as it climbed up and crushed
the backs of deep green waves.
On waking, he sees fire flies
swaying and bobbing out of
the night's lapping mouth.
Gathered at the docks,
they become boats seeking lines.
He feels his own tied
to his hands, his feet, as if he's
web-bound and stretched above his host.
He breaks for the deck, sets free his lines;
unfurls and raises his ghost.

ONE-SIDED ARGUMENT WITH THE NIGHT

In the evening my eyes find
a sky of burning periods.
The moon isn't a completed sentence.
The air is limp as a sail in irons.
Because it is so immense,
the lake holds up my boat.
But it won't allow me to walk
on its slate black water.
From this anchorage to the shore
is the distance from my heart
to the Evening Star.
There is no way to reason
with the air, with Venus,
or the fickle water, no way
for my heart to convince the stars,
so immense they hold up everything,
to let me walk to shore tonight,
to let me find some music,
share some light.

ROWING TO THE OTHER SIDE

Mist rolls along the hull.
My boat sweats to slippery decks.
Invited over, I've rowed across
the water's black surface,
where, below the fog,
the stars twitch and waver.
Their boat is moored in
the intimate lapping of the sky.
A tiny light in the cabin
and a pale arm extend in welcome.
I board and the skipper's daughter
offers me a beer from below.
Stories are traded about her
and her crew of brothers.
Their laughter disappears in the fog.
Then the skipper douses his cigar
and reminds them of the evil season
when the mast snapped suddenly,
crashed among them, rigging and spars
snagging them, pulling them over the side;
the froth-peaked waves caressing
their necks, numbing their legs.
The survivors sink into quiet stares.
In the damp silence, an owl calls,
the moon, the moon, the moon.
We'd all seen it like a broken port light
roving over the rippled sky.
We peer up as if to see
the Little Dipper wheel away,
drawing the fog up over the water's surface
'til it's hard to sight the other boats.
We are ghosts in these cold clouds.

Shivering, we say good-bye.
I row across the universe
toward my invisible home.
We sleep this night beneath the mercy
of rigging and spars, while all the world
sinks below the stars.

FINDING THE CENTER

A ghost of salt
in the sea's clothes,
I jerked down the jib.
The wind beat me
until my jacket and sweater
dissolved into rags.
A second reef in the mainsail,
next would be to lower.
I held on and made way.
The sea was a thunderstorm
and rained down on me.
The wind forced water
down my throat, made me think.
A wave put me over the toerail,
my head a howl within my mouth.
Over the hull's glassy curve
I saw the heavy center,
a wing erupting from the water
like a drowning angel.

SEARCHING FOR A MOORING

A tiny breeze,
its pressure and voice
cold and wet
on my face,
an astringent
for my eyes.
A variety of slow noise
in waves on rocks,
waves on hull,
waves on buoys.
The surface up here
no better
than the hidden bottom—
untrodden mud,
an end for blind sailors.
I rely on local knowledge.
But it fails me
as a sudden boat
condenses a foot off
the starboard rail.
But she is already moored
to the underworld.
I feel my way around her
back into the fog,
alone in my search
for my own place below.

COMING HOME

Coming in at night
I listen for the shoal's
lapping tongues or
the cove's
heavy breath
along the cooling point.
Then I get a light
to mark the buoys,
cold bobbing men
in black water.
The breeze keeps
the insects away as
I make her secure.
Lying back in the cockpit
I hear how the mast acts
as a ground for the stars,
conducting their music
down to the water, to me.
The boat works her lines,
and I slip under the night
into a big walnut tree,
its huge limbs outspread,
hands holding up the sky.
Tiny lights rise from the lawn.
In a truck tire roped to the tree,
I sprawl drowsy as it rocks
easy in the breeze like a boat
moored to the earth.
I have always slept
with the music of stars
and stretching lines.

THIS IS WHERE

the great black hole of the world
comes to drink beyond the moonlit reef,
out where air is born breaking waves
below the clicking palms. The stars fail
at filling all this space with light.
Their grief floats on the ocean's face
like the dreams of fish that trouble
the bobbing hearts of sailors.
High on the sand where the house rests
a man pulls the cords that bathe
the walls and floors in night. This is where
the great black hole of the world comes
to drink beyond the moonlit reef,
where I walk naked to the edge of the sea
and implacably let the tide dissolve my grief.

IN THE MUD ACCEPTING SOME LIGHT

This night the moon is old,
decayed to darkness.
Stars lose their leftover light
that was old when her attendants
buried Queen Shub-ad under Ur,
head pillowed, eyes closed
to her attendants beyond the door
preparing to accompany her.
The girls who'd served her gave up
their light below as she grew ancient
as the moon and the moon's absence.
They all waited, wise fossils, patiently
to rise from the desert in dusty hands.
In this muddy field and spring grass
where all assume the dark's disguise,
I raise my arms to the stars till my lungs
break open and my heart scrapes
against my chest like a rusty spade.
I raise my arms in welcome to the light
of the living stars and the dead stars,
and the light of the old moon.

RUNNING AGROUND

The lighter water to each side
marks the darker channel,
but I'm thinking about a woman
and how she uses time.
It's not like striking a rock,
all the noise and tipping,
but soft, a lift,
like the bottom takes a breath.
The mud embraces
my every maneuver.
The woman I think of
is like all the other boats,
off in the distance.
I sit alone on the bow;
imagine how, the earth run aground,
gravity choked,
this woman
would float up,
no more appointments,
lunches, or forsythia
to chop out and root kill.
It would lift my keel.
She stops the yard work, now;
the keel drags free
like cuttings to the curb,
and the bow returns
to dark green swells.
The water is unwilling to fantasize.
I am pushed deeper into mud.

where I will open my coat
and share my warmth
and let my blood and breath be
my companions in the world.

THE DELICIOUS RELEASE OF LOVELY SORROW

Let the sun-sunk colors
of the sky and the
foraging rabbit's eye
gather the darkness
of this night.

Let the dog on the snowed
path, the small copper
bell on his collar,
be the song of a
cold angel's omen.

Let the empty tracks
of boots in the
powdery ice be all
the ghosts who
now avoid me.

When the rabbit has
vanished in the underbrush
and the dog disappeared
from the path, I am left alone
to finish the walk to the cabin
where I will open my coat
and share my warmth
and let my blood and breath be
my companions in the world.

THE ANGEL UNDER THE TREE

I found it, after walking the dogs,
crashed out next to my elm.
Cracked, papery wings cradled its shell
like a thin stainless-steel bowl.
The black mirrors of its eyes
were frosted by stars.
The ragged nails of winter air
had pierced its surfaces.
Later in the night, after making love,
I went back out into the cold
and wept over the mess
my heart had murdered.
I slid the dark wreck under the tree.
Perhaps the tree's insulated life
could bless its tiny, monstrous bones.
Once I told a woman about its misshapen body,
like an exotic bird, somehow escaped
into winter's blade; that I had found it,
smoothed its frozen feathers
and buried it among the roots
that groped after its banished brothers.

POEM FOR THE HARD OF HEARING

She says she opened
herself for him.
He says he entered
herself for her.
Their hands play
with blood that feeds
a measure of time.
Afterward, she whispers
and he imagines
the wall whispers.
And it does.
Sighs rush through
openings in the chilly house
but neither of them
can hear
the soft, inexorable
rubbing of empty limbs
on the bedroom window.

THE TASTE I KEEP

For Susan

I see the early
edge of light seep
in and soften you.
Without a finger
I touch you now.

The scent of your wiry
hair where your heart
joins your legs
slept in my palm,
in my thoughtless hand.

Awake your eyes gather
all available light.
But I breathe in how
smooth you feel asleep,
the muscles you shared,
the taste I keep.

WHAT IT'S LIKE TO DRIVE WITH
A SLEEPING WOMAN

She breathes the noise of wheels
on damp concrete. Headlights
are what disturb her—
the ex-husband's eyes
penetrate the streaked glass.
Nothing can protect her
from the gravel's chatter
or the warning of silence.
She's not ready to wake up
in Dodge City, she's not ready
to drop out of the car
into any man's arms.

AFTER SHE BOUGHT A NEW HUMIDIFIER

She called to tell me
a white powder settled
on her possessions as she slept.
I told her it was my shadow's residue,
a nuisance, true, like my painting
still hanging on her west wall.
She had asked me over and over,
did I want it back?
She hadn't trusted the gift
to be a proper gentleman.
It watches her drag her clothes off
in the evenings, watches
as the night gown with the lace
flower at the neck settles
over her shoulders, catches
on her chilly nipples.
It told me only what I'd seen before.
I've removed her picture
from my dresser, put it in the drawer
with directions to other elegant machines
no longer working, but I still
wrap the scarf she gave me
around my throat. I trust it.
It is brown
and dry like plans
embodied in autumn leaves.

WAKE-UP CALL

I wake up in a hotel room
and think it is my home
and though I've traveled
hundreds of miles, I've never left.
The woman in bed next to me
isn't the woman I wanted to take,
but the woman who came with me,
though both are the same.
Her eyes are not clenched
against the sun but against me
and my desire.
I think she wants to touch me,
but she always carries the laundry,
the paperwork and the exhaustion
of all the invention.
Tomorrow will look much the same.
So I watch her board a plane,
see her eyes relax as she gazes
from her window seat as I dissolve.
She is unable to wave good-bye.
The jet slips sideways
toward the imperfect sky.

I will stay in this cabin
on the snow-sunk hillside
til all my ink runs out
and I can draw no more women.

WATCHING A WOMAN TYPE

Something familiar about the light,
about her arm briefly
extended under the low lamp;
her fine hair; tiny pores that help
her breathe. Something familiar about
the veins, where they ease down
between her fingers;
the ball of her elbow in shadow.
A ring leans against a knuckle.
Something familiar about her shirt,
where its wrinkles gather under her arm.
The sleeve trembles
over her softest curve. Something familiar
suggests my dead wife's lines of light.
But this is a living woman,
the mark on her face
of the earth's heavy center,
a beautiful darkness under each eye.
I celebrate the simple pleasure
of this bas relief through my eyes only.
Familiar shadows on the surface of night.

DESIRE

Inside, I imagine a ceiling fan
easily stirs the air into comfort.
Outside, the sun's patterns
burn my shortest shadow.
At the doorstep, I search
for an opening, it's a long task.
The old world is behind me,
the summer is at my back;
too short, too hot, all I can
carry through the door is
the urge to taste your pulse.
I'm still searching at the door;
I came all this way and
I may never reach home.

VENGEANCE OVER FAITH

I will stay in this cabin
on the snow-sunk hillside
till all my ink runs out
and I can draw no more women,
till all my pencil leads are
ground into paper as words
into this wooden silence,
till all the hard candy
has dissolved on my tongue
like love dissolves in my dreams,
till my water jug is empty
as my bed, blankets peeled back
to reveal the same white
that buries my tracks.
I will stay in this cabin
on the snow-sunk hillside
till I know every lover
has lost her way,
till I burn the drawings and words,
my tongue melting snow
instead of the faith
that curves dark between your legs.

AFTERNIGHT ON THE ISLAND

The sea is love's rough surgeon
and the sea-moon is a shattered glass,
like the one I dashed on black coral,
then surf-bashed gathered pieces.
I wrapped my fingers in a rag,
but still red glazes this new glass.
Its rim rests on my lip,
the sea reflected in its bottom.
The rum goes down, the sea follows.
Foolishly, I lick my own fingers
for some salt, a taste of skin.

How many worlds are broken
with a coconut's husking and opening,
but can I survive without its milky light?
Cries of little crimes slit the air
every morning as parrots beak
and squabble like brutal butterflies.
For such injuries there is nothing
the sea or anyone else can do.
Foolishly, I lick my own fingers
for salt, a taste of skin, of blood.
I am an echo amusing itself
against the tile floors, the stucco walls.

The smooth curve of your belly becomes moonlight

YOUR SMALL FINGERS AND THEIR SMALL BONES

For Maryfrances

Now I think of you—
your small fingers
and their small bones;
your large eyes opened wide
to encompass
the full moon as it passed
above the island; it was clean
and white like the skin
above your breasts, the skin
unsullied by the sun;
your brown arms, how they
pushed back the night air,
how they came
to rest on my shoulders;
the warmth of you,
like the day's heat
had settled in every cell,
in your small fingers
and their small bones;
the heat that rose
above the island and
the easy trades
that blew it away,
the heat that sank
into your hair; that
I could hold you
as I held the colors
of the sea in my heart;

that I could taste
the same salt
that sparkled on your thighs
as you walked from the water
and raised your hand,
your small brown fingers
and their small lovely bones.

LOOKING AT YOU

Glancing into the body of darkness
resting on the road's shoulder,
suddenly I am looking at you,
having lost yourself on my tongue's tip,
winding your face and chest within
the sheets. The smooth curve
of your belly becomes moonlight.

In the museum transfixed
by Kirckner's portrait of Franzi,
suddenly I am looking at you,
having lost yourself in the green glass
of the ocean's edge, the wind pulling
your sun dress—a transparent veil
across your breasts. Your eyes
focused on the breaking seas.

Watching children escape barefoot
on the dark street into lamplight,
suddenly I am looking at you,
having lost yourself at rummaging
in your bureau drawer; naked
in the streetlight, inducing the delicate
edge of your shoulder, the underside
of your breast, the palm-fitting
turn of your ass, to glow in
the lapping fan-cooled air.

Like a small animal being hunted,
I am lucky your beauty is not focused
only on me, but ranges free
on the edges of light, the graceful
surfaces of the sea. I wish to remain
hidden until every bulb in the house
has burned out. And then suddenly,
I'll be looking at you, looking at me.

AT HER LOVER'S APPROACH

She stands before her reflection,
brushing her hair,
her loose hand in the air,
her index finger pointing
lackadaisical at the other
in the mirror.
Her eyes follow the brush
whose bristles sing
like a mother shushing
her sleepy child—
shush, shush, shush,
they glide like black blades
separating filaments of night.
The other in the glass
follows the bristles too.
She cannot hear their song,
nor the lover's approach
in the hall, a whisper.
For a moment their eyes lock,
the other and the real,
gauging lines and creases
like worried engineers;
then she brings the brush down
and the other disappears.

WHY WE SOMETIMES JOIN HANDS

Like agitated dogs
winter rushes around
the house, and inside
we breathe the cost
of cold, dry air.
We're in the basement
loading laundry and her
housecoat falls open.
Like small hands, her
breasts hold in life.
Below ground looking up,
looking out through
a tiny window, up at the
naked trees whose lives
have gone underground
too, we join hands.

LIKE ANOTHER STORM THE WORLD
TURNS THROUGH

It's not right
that I leave you tonight,
more like a thief than a lover.
As I file my muscles
into the moonlight,
the miserly clouds hide it
like an empty exclamation.
If the wind builds against the towers
with their red lights,
broken signals will fall soft
as the lashes that fold
across your eyes.
I will be lost.
For now, I make my way,
smell and taste you still,
in the rush of hands in my head
like another storm
the world turns through.

ALL THAT YOU THOUGHT

I tell you now,
all that you thought
was worth your eyes
and the contents
of your sweet shaped skull
is nothing when I watch
the breath that pushes
your breasts against
the sheet as you tally
items that will find
a home for your hands.
I should wake you, say *stop*,
kiss your fingers, tell you
that cycle of sighs
is what pushes the planets
through my juices, brings
my blood up the wick
and my tongue to your fingertips.

IF I THINK OF A WOMAN

It's twilight and the birds sing
as if it's sunrise. Their song sounds
like groggy afterthoughts, a welcome
to the night. They celebrate the colors
evaporated out of all that breathes,
relishing sleep beneath the sky.
Or perhaps they complain
like tired children, how they refuse
to relinquish beauty. I've sung
my own complaints of beauties
that cease to speak.
If I think of a woman, I see her;
a small animal secure in her fur,
listening to my song. I see her
naked in dim light talking
about hands, how they touch her.
She talks about skin, how it fits her,
how it heats under fingers.
If I think of a woman, I see sunrise;
hear birds welcome sight;
glimpse her brown, short-cropped hair;
hear my song change to include the light.

A LONG DRIVE HOME

The dusky sky is so empty
it becomes an anchor,
inhabits my windshield
and holds the car fast.
The world continues to roll
back under my tires
bringing signs:
a squirrel caught hustling
in the highway's middle—
the fresh yellow centerline
painted across his belly.
A hill barges under the hood
and I crest into the side
of a phantom tractor
lurched from a fallen corn forest.
All this goes against the grain
of the heartbeat beading up
red behind my eyes.
So I peel back these portents
and conjure you as you step
from a steaming tub,
nipples coiling up in cool air,
their hard red points
and your green eyes
make a simple constellation.
I can taste you, warm and salty.
Now the car begins to move,
to break through the static night,
to deliver me to that little sea.
I get my fingers wet
and kiss the stars.

AFTER READING GATSBY

Before I knew the fragrance
of her spine in sweat
or washed her back,
I stood at my boat's bow,
and watched a green light,
distant, dissolve in the night.
Her dream was cool water
I slipped into, a dark solution,
boundless; it soothed
through the hull as I slept
below the chime of halyards.
If visions were true entities,
we would meet above the water
and evaporate into the stars.
For a summer she meandered
along the beach, looked for treasures.
She crouched on the sand peering out
above the sea. She wished not
for a light; she wished for me.

WITNESS

I hear more and more
about the deer, how they stumble
upon synthetic wood settlements,
wander through backyards,
eat from the trees
that now belong to someone.
At school, the custodian tells me,
twenty crossed the highway
as if fleeing the slow wave of winter dusk,
the traffic stopped,
children jeered from windows.
The skittish drivers like fidgeting voyeurs.
Out where farmland and windbreak
become the edges of empires,
an acquaintance points as a giant loader
tears trees out of the soil.
Animals plague her garden.
The deer can't stay
on their own turf.
Saturday afternoon, I watch a small herd
file through our tiny backwoods.
A doe scans the hill as they hurry
into thinning trees.
I feel the way I did the first time
I saw my wife's naked body
edged in moonlight
from the bedroom's canopied window.
It was midnight, the street out front, silent,
no one else to see the pale curves
immersed in shadows.
I watched her scan the window
before crossing into the broken dark
and saw what was never meant for my selfish eyes.

HER HEART'S SMALL PURSE OF MAGIC

Some of my most calm moments
are spent holding my love
and cupping her breast's
supple weight, small and sharp,
as if it contains her heart,
its least rhythm caresses my palm.
It's fragile but firm in all that rests
in its chimeric tissues.
It's her sweet breath inhaled
to its peak and then released slowly,
softly to my lips
across a million years.

I curled in the floorboard pocket below
and looked up at the bulk of its curves.

ON A COLD EVENING, ALONE, I TURN ON
MY ELECTRIC BLANKET

I dreamed myself into the back
of my father's '55 Buick.
Under his big bass fiddle,
I curled in the floorboard pocket below
and looked up at the bulk of its curves.
Its neck rested on the seat,
projected into the air between my parents.
My brother took his turn
in the pocket behind the driver
as I took mine resting my ear
on the hum of the drive tunnel—
lullaby of metal spinning in air.
Above us on the seat, my sister,
wrapped in army surplus blankets.
The warmth of the heater
under my father's seat was dry and sharp
as the broken snow beneath us.
Delicate as the ice fog
that dissolved the world,
we were all poised on the edge of sleep.
I raised myself up till I could look down
the big fiddle's neck to its scrolled head
pointed toward Alaska.
I could feel the emptiness inside it
and I could feel the possibilities
stretched tight above its fragile lacquered skin.
I watched my mother's head lean
toward my father's shoulder
as she leaned into the night
that rushed at us outside the windshield.
He hummed a show tune
as the moon burst through
the fog like a spotlight.

The glowing dashboard fired the edges
of my mother's hair
and I felt that the warm steel shell
around us would find its way
through miles of frozen air,
would carry these instruments home.

THE MAN IN THE NEXT ROOM COUGHS

It's a cough small and soft, though he's alone
in there, no one to disturb but me drowsing
in my identical room. It's an intimate cough
like those heard in a trenchcoated crowd
outside an all-night movie house. Cold air
scrapes hungry throats and they cough.
Behind their hands they file in to watch
a woman, pink, out of focus, run
the delicate tines of her fingers, a carved bone
comb through her pubic hair. The men cough
an abrupt, aching cough, each man in a row
of empty seats. The man in the next room now
coughs two packs of Camels and a case
of Pabst Blue Ribbon a day. A familiar cough.
I dream the wall between us is my childhood
bedroom's wall. I sit on my squat bed, listen
to my father cough in the dark. My mother
rustles the bedsheets in answer. I hear his
weight question the bed, a cough from behind
his hand. Then, another stifled cough; a ridge
above the farm pond I find him sighting
his rifle on a groundhog. He pulls the trigger;
the animal's skull neatly splits. My father turns
smoothly like a rifle bolt, sees me staring,
starts to speak and coughs again.
The man in the next room coughs. I wake
on my back in this unfamiliar bed; clear my throat,
low, to myself, feel memories short of air drag
in my lungs. The man in the next room coughs.
I sit up and answer deep in my throat,
my affection, deep in this night.

THE END OF TRUSTING HER

Good Friday Earthquake,
Anchorage, Alaska, 1964

The mud beaches buckled
and brought the Cook Inlet's waves
beneath the bluffs, the houses
and buildings, the trees,
the people who peered at their feet,
tried to see the invisible storm.
Working in the basement,
I heard the thunder approach,
saw the storm waves rise
in the concrete, peaks burst
in a spray of sharp chips.
A subterranean wind
snaked the stairs and every nail,
every board complained.
Through a screeching window,
I saw 30-foot pines whip the snow.
The storm loosed ink-black cracks
to gallop, to shatter the pure white lens,
to split trees like old clothespins.
I saw it wasn't the end of the Earth
but the end of trusting her.
She'd had a dream of stormy resurrection,
opened up to spit out her spirits,
swallowed a few of her surface brood.
Later, in foul weather gear,
we went down into her rumbling lair
to reclaim those who still bled
and gasped for her air.

GETTING SAVED

Good Friday Earthquake,
Anchorage, Alaska, 1964

Their blades brought wind
to burn my face, slice my eyes.
Helicopters descended on the streets,
on the skating rink;
some hovered, waiting above the snow.
I saw my father down in a crack,
down in the permafrost earth
with other men pulling
one of my school friends out.
He was a broken boy in a broken world.
Two men rolled him into a blanket.
They passed him along a line
to the rhythm of the blades above them.
Strapped onto a stretcher, his body ascended.
Above, I saw his foot, over the side,
dangling by raw meat and tendons.
I ran toward the rising helicopter,
pointed up, shouted about his leg, his foot;
the blood spewed, rained down in prop wash.
I waved my arms at the pilot, but my friend
rose mechanically into the confused,
bloody chaos of salvation.

ARSHILE GORKY AVOIDS THE WAR

He steps through the doorway
but his mother and sister
remain seated to either side
of the end table forever.
In the small dooryard,
in the small village of Kourkom,
he leans out for a view of the road
and stumbles over a Turkish helmet.
Falling face down in the grass,
Arshile Gorky's head continues deeper
till his eyes are pierced by the blades.
Later, in a skiff, he is rowed to Patras
sitting stiff as a quill
on a floating carcass, his eyes
still stabbed with green.
He believes at first his dream
is insubstantial, his desire wanton.
In New York he holds his brush
to his throat like a dirty knife.
His love withers, his talent grows.
Later, in a Buick, he is driven to Martha's Vineyard.
Pollock opens a bottle of Jack Daniel's easily,
they share it.
Finding himself in the woodshed,
Arshile, who did not skin his knees,
who missed Babi Yar—
finally hangs quietly.

MY FAMILY HAS ARSHILE GORKY FOR DINNER

Strangely enough
his head is not tough
but rather tender.
My father says *let me try*
one of those arms
making a big C
around the biceps with his forefinger and thumb.
My sister gazes for a while
at his crotch,
then toys with the table linen.
My mother points out
she is moody, then joins my sister glumly.
My brother demands wings, drumsticks,
sings for his supper—
Gum-ooh Mow Mow!
But they all find
most of Arshile much too hard to chew.
The whole table looks at me now.
I'm the one who cut him down.

SOME IMPOSSIBLY FLY

On the trail to Lower Russian Lake
the air was dark and the river talked
to the wind in the high trees.
Near the bank, thunder began
to breathe a mist that settled
in the ears like an answer.
When I heard it, I broke away
from my father, ran to the spongy edge
high above the tumbling current.
The falls, like a cross of water,
bore dog salmon and flecks of blood.
My father called me back,
but I climbed over the edge.
Thighs and back beaten by the rocks,
I watched the fish beat themselves
to death, some impossibly fly
above the falls, an offering of silver.
I saw the fish pass through the veil;
I wished to pass through, too,
but the cataract would not let me.
My boot slipped; I slid into thunder.
My nails ripped at stones.
Then, balanced above me,
my father's hand descended.

WHAT SLEEP MEANS

You let go and slammed into the floor.
It was not soft and wet like your bed.
Exhaustion was your step-mother.
In her heavy arms she enfolded you
and fed you liquid spirits.
She loved you and you could not
get enough, her love fluttered up
around you like a thousand
hungry starlings, black and green
flashing across your lidded eyes.
Together we found you guilty
of everything, but in the mess
on the rug we found you innocent.
In some dreams I discovered
forgiveness resides in the eyes,
shifting like wheeling flights
of blackbirds, it eases the lids shut,
and the invisible weight of leaving
locks them shut forever.
Those late-night gigs taught me
the night was my step-mother,
the moon was my drug of choice,
its light seeping through me
like the bitter glow of good whiskey.
The sodium glow of pain, this fall night,
snaps on all the way down the road
and stutters off again when the fire rises.
How innocent you rested in the center
of the floor, breathing your own vomit,
splashing in that acid and learning how
to swim again like you taught me:
carried to the cove and thrown in
I awoke into water, into struggle,
and the strokes of salvation.

Now we are both saved, though not
by any god, but by the ineffable laws
of sleep, the leaving, the waking,
the rising, the tired slide under grace.

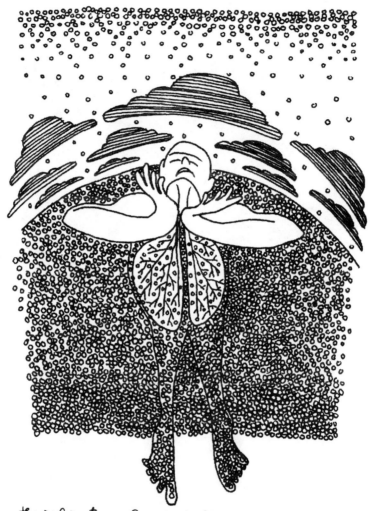

the red roots and afterbirth of words

ANOTHER GHOST STORY

Call me Ishmael, or Luke, or John, or William.
I am no better or worse than Ahab,
though a captain carries a great responsibility,
the ship and all its souls at the mercy of the world.
We are all one and the same, we all searched.
It took time, too, but other than the sea,
none of us were vexed alone, but with each other.
All animals crowded tooth and jowl
on that leaking, sinking ship.
I can say that I found the whale.
I found the whale, though in truth, it was not white.
There was no mythical struggle.
I tracked it down and killed it.
It sank below the blue, heaving earth, a mile down
where the sun can never touch it.
There at the cold bottom of my heart it rots, slowly.
It could be years before nothing is left
but the stained leviathan of its bones.
And those, too, will sink deep in that red mud.
It is so easy to kill, so hard to live with the corpse.
All the other boys aboard? Their names I've borrowed
when it helped. Living or dead, we drift in this world
hidden from each other, alone with the imperceptible
pulse of all our murders.

THE MASS

We carry our lungs, breathing hard;
this world's air in two heavy sacks,
the red roots and afterbirth of words
in two heavy bags.
We're ashamed, stumbling
and barely capable
of carrying our thick, ropy legs
and splayed feet.
We see in a dream
that clay is really mud.
Our father told us
a good man's pride
could grow in his arms,
but ours only ache
as we carry headfulls of visions.
We are wearing out with this work.
To carry our lives,
these bays of clouds
like a vast, dark pinwheel
spoked into the low distance,
is to spin heavily and headlong
in the wind of the sun and sea.
These large wet messes of living meat,
the weight of our lives, our deaths,
our sagging souls, crunches through
the leaves of trees and starlight.
If we were as meager and dry,
we could drift and tumble a good mile.
If we were as meager and dry,
we would not have to be sunk
so heavily into the ground,
the whispered lies settling over
the prepared baggage, the mass.

I laid their heads to the east
so their spirits could see
the daylight reborn
as the stars back away for awhile.

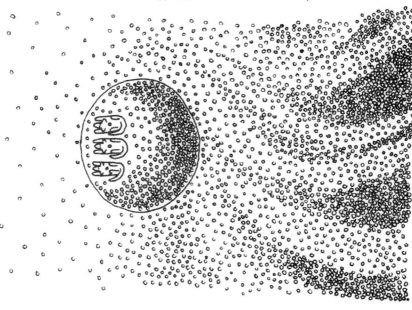

CHILDREN AND STONES

When we are children
walking the path
and stop, to bend,
to pick up a pretty stone,
there is in the motion
an assent, yes, time allows it.
Later, we might put the stone
in a small blue matchbox
gently, like a kiss
to the back of our skulls
put there by our fondest lover.
It appears to us for years,
this pretty stone,
revealed in frantic hunts,
in headachy sortings,
ticking like a clock.
We lose it, find it,
and lose it again,
like an obscure pain
beneath the tips of our hearts.
Our own hearts
that beat roughly
until they're beaten into dust.
Then someone else discovers
the small blue box
with its quiet, pretty stone.
Someone else examines
the stone's exotic surface.
The stone is tossed
into the air like a coin
and then tossed out the door.
Someone whispers to oneself,
so that is love:
children and stones.

AFTER WATCHING A MAN PLAYING
WITH HIS DOG IN THE GRASS

I have buried three dogs in two years.
Three dogs as old as my heart.
I laid their heads to the east
so their spirits could see
the daylight reborn
as the stars back away for a while.

Before, I held their heads in my hands
to comfort them, to let them take
some of me in with their grateful tongues.
I played the part of the gods,
called death in over the black lines.
She came bearing a plastic syringe.
I do not believe they saw that
as weakness, but perhaps, wondered
why pain had occupied their bones
and the world kept bumping their heads.
They barely saw what my gentle hands brought.

Those ceremonies were bittersweet and common,
as common as making love in summer
with the air-conditioning broken down,
slipping toward that liquid state,
a heaviness in the groin of our best
effort at changing the weather.
That storm brings the rain
and it slowly dissolves us.
It runs and drips down our softening skin,
cooling our fur. The storm
brings the sudden glorious wind,
sweet as the first contraction
that speeds us out into the light
or releases the first of the universe
into the emptiness of night.

THIS LIFE AND NO OTHER

For instance, the wind splashes through leaves
and the leaves drip down, yellowed pages, old letters.
Mornings, fog sits on the ground, heavy
as a cinematic bad dream, hiding icy grass.
Late afternoons, crickets sing of luck,
and a storm of good fortune glides above you
like torn sails loose in the sky.
You can't find the sheets or halyards to control them,
to bring them down.
The dogs are risqué, mounting each other all day.
Evenings, tree frogs finish up the story.
None of this eases the crickets in your legs
or the snake of your loins.
It's like driving on the freeway
when ahead you see hills recede
into a joyous gray, one might mistake
for the end of the day.
But it's just the dirty air or a thunder storm,
a common trick, and you must drive beyond it
to dry your wings in the sun.

Greg Field

Greg Field is an artist, writer, and educator who lives in Independence, Missouri. His paintings are in several private collections all over the country. His poems have been published in many journals and anthologies. He has been an instructor or presenter at seminars and workshops on poetry writing throughout Missouri and the Mid-West.

Andrea Brookhart

Andrea Brookhart is a Kansas City artist who currently works at Hallmark Cards as a digital designer. Her background includes a BFA in painting from the University of Kansas and twenty years experience in the printing and publishing industry.